'enérgeia

Composition
Via
Photograph

Patrick A Drake

"An object in motion tends to remain in motion along a straight line unless acted upon by an outside force." — Isaac Newton

WHAT IS MATHEMATICS?

Stars illuminate
Exhilarate moons
To know beauty
Infinite via

TIME MACHINE

Connection

ACT I

Gabriella awakens and proceeds to the river to gather water but she never returns.

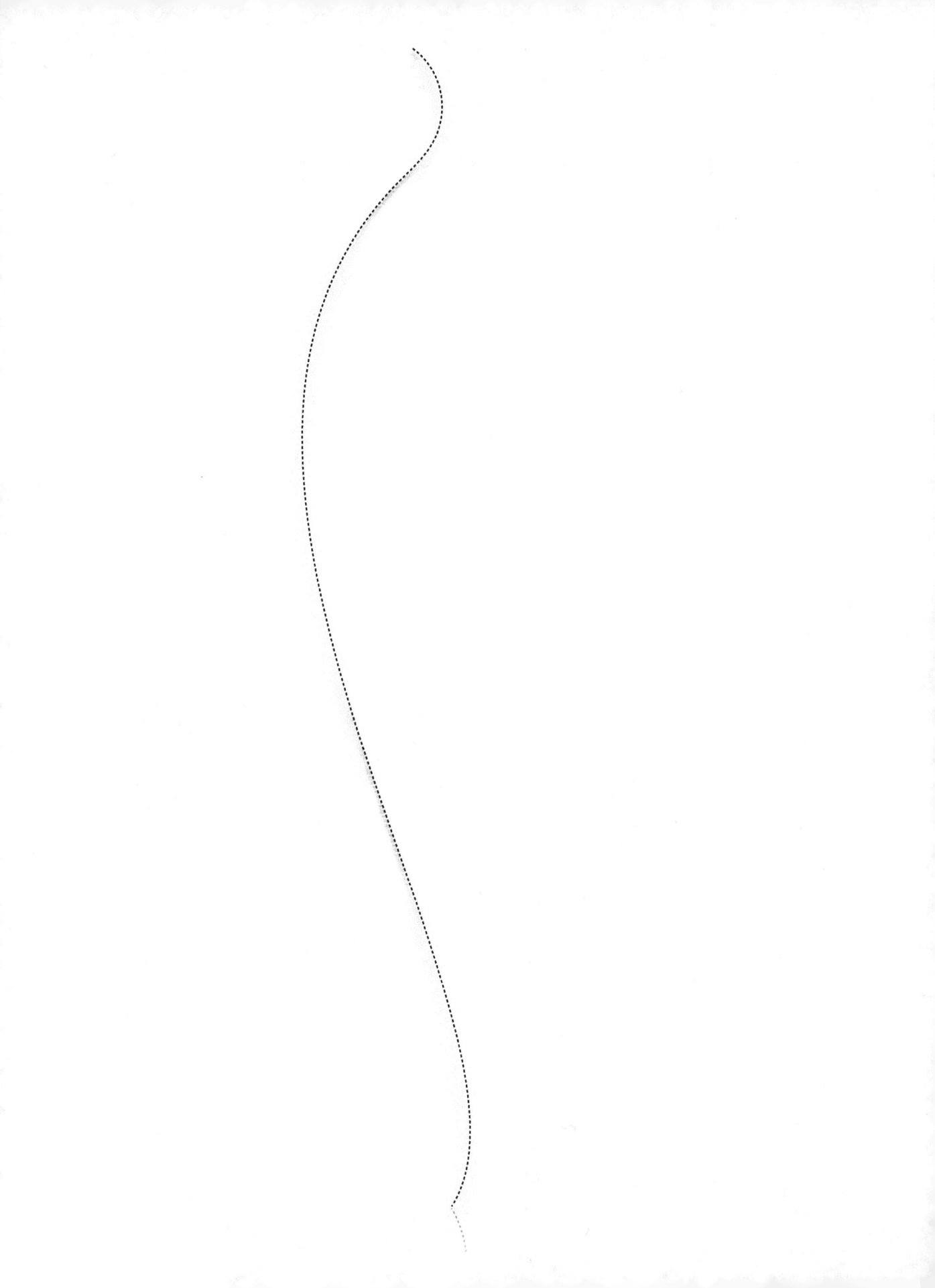

Act II

Jericho can no longer suffer waiting for Gabriella to return, a journey begins.

INT. *Lufthansa*

JERICHO

I gazed upon the Dragon, fearsome; unable to move, unable to speak, unable to scream.

INT. *Lufthansa*

Date	Departure	Arrival	Flight	Dura-tion	Cabin
Mon 8 Sep	**17:55** Atlanta	09:10 +1 Frankfurt	LH445	22h50	Business (Z)
Tue 9 Sep	17:50 Frankfurt	**01:15 +1** Tehran , Imam Khomeini Interna-tional	LH600		Business (Z)
Thu 18 Sep	**03:05** Tehran, Imam Khomeini Interna-tional	06:00 Frankfurt	LH601	21h15	Business (Z)
Thu 18 Sep	11:45 Frankfurt	**15:50** Atlanta	LH444		Business (Z)

Jericho enters the cabin to find his seat occupied by a precarious, stunning woman frocked in academia.

INT. *Lufthansa*

                          JERICHO

                          Forgive me

                          WOMAN

                          (composed)

                          SOPHIA

INT. *Lufthansa*

                         SOPHIA

        It is truth not name that inspires one's destiny

                         JERICHO

         Phenomenal, a professor of platitudes

INT. *Lufthansa*

Immediately after Jericho sits, he prays.

                        JERICHO

*Order is the best good reward there is. There are wished-for things in the wish for this one
when one's Order is for the best Order.*

INT. *Lufthansa*

JERICHO

There is one that exists constant

.

INT. *Lufthansa*

> SOPHIA

At what point does discipline become the essence of the flower?

> JERICHO

Precision.

INT. *Lufthansa*

JERICHO

Subjective move in thoughts and dreams, objective,

darkness.

INT. *Lufthansa*

JERICHO

Travel is not Point A to Point B but beginning to beginning.

We embark within the abstract.

INT. *Lufthansa*

JERICHO

I surmise mystery is reality.

SOPHIA

Chaos

Act III

Jericho is introduced to the work of Sophia and he is inspired by the science of time.

INT. *Elementary classroom*

Students listen intensely as they are read a story by their teacher. One boy's attention is curiously focused solely outside of the classroom window.

                              TEACHER

                              Jericho

                              JERICHO

                              Listen

The teacher and students all focus on the outside of the classroom window bewildered.

INT. *The CIA Office of General Counsel (OGC)*

NARRATOR

Tonight, on FRONTLINE: An investigation of the CIA and its role in international drug dealing.

INT. *CIA Office of General Counsel (OGC)*

COUNSEL

One must recognize the distinction in news, media, press.

INT. Embassy of Switzerland

No. 39, Shahid Mousavi (Golestan 5th)

Corner of Paidarfard St. (ex-Amir Ebrahimi St.)

Pasdaran

Tehran

A consular relations specialist within the Foreign Interests Section receives an e-mail that sparks a calm frenzy.

SPECIALIST

(reading)

Free 'enérgeia

$(0,1)$

center $(0,0)$

radius $= 1$

$x^2 + y^2 = 1$

$\frac{2\pi}{4}$

$(-\frac{1}{2}, \frac{\sqrt{3}}{2})$

$(-\frac{\sqrt{2}}{2}, \frac{\sqrt{2}}{2})$

$t = \frac{2\pi}{3}$

$t = \frac{3\pi}{4}$

$t = \frac{\pi}{2}$

$(\frac{1}{2}, \frac{\sqrt{3}}{2})$

$t = \frac{\pi}{3}$

$t = \frac{\pi}{4}$

$(\frac{\sqrt{2}}{2}, \frac{\sqrt{2}}{2})$

$= 2\pi \approx 6.28$

$(-\frac{\sqrt{3}}{2}, \frac{1}{2})$ $t = \frac{5\pi}{6}$

$t = \frac{\pi}{6}$ $(\frac{\sqrt{3}}{2}, \frac{1}{2})$

$(-1, 0)$

$t = \pi$

$(1, 0)$

$t = 0, 2\pi$ $\frac{8\pi}{4}$

$\frac{\sqrt{3}}{2}, -\frac{1}{2})$

$t = \frac{7\pi}{6}$

$t = \frac{11\pi}{6}$ $(\frac{\sqrt{3}}{2}, -$

$\frac{\sqrt{2}}{2}, \frac{-\sqrt{2}}{2})$ $t = \frac{5\pi}{4}$

$t = \frac{4\pi}{3}$

$t = \frac{3\pi}{2}$

$t = \frac{5\pi}{3}$

$t = \frac{7\pi}{4}$ $(\frac{\sqrt{2}}{2}, \frac{-\sqrt{2}}{2})$

$(-\frac{1}{2}, -\frac{\sqrt{3}}{2})$

$(0, -1)$

$(\frac{1}{2}, -\frac{\sqrt{3}}{2})$

www.ingramcontent.com/pod-product-compliance
Lightning Source LLC
Chambersburg PA
CBHW081315170526
45166CB00011B/3534